NATIVE AMERICAN

FOOD

FROM SALMON TO SUCCOTASH

BY MELISSA RAÉ SHOFNER

Gareth Stevens
PUBLISHING

Please visit our website, www.garethstevens.com. For a free color catalog of all our high-quality books, call toll free 1-800-542-2595 or fax 1-877-542-2596.

Library of Congress Cataloging-in-Publication Data

Names: Shofner, Melissa Raé, author.
Title: Native American food : from salmon to succotash / Melissa Raé Shofner.
Description: New York : Gareth Stevens Publishing, 2018. | Series: Native
  American cultures | Includes bibliographical references and index.
Identifiers: LCCN 2017029738| ISBN 9781538208762 (paperback) | ISBN
  9781538208779 (6 pack) | ISBN 9781538208786 (library bound)
Subjects: LCSH: Indians of North America–Food–Juvenile literature. | Indian
  cooking–Juvenile literature.
Classification: LCC E98.F7 S56 2018 | DDC 641.59/297–dc23
LC record available at https://lccn.loc.gov/2017029738

First Edition

Published in 2018 by
Gareth Stevens Publishing
111 East 14th Street, Suite 349
New York, NY 10003

Copyright © 2018 Gareth Stevens Publishing

Designer: Sarah Liddell
Editor: Therese Shea

Photo credits: Cover, p. 1 (main image) Jeff Greenberg/Contributor/Universal Images Group/ Getty Images; cover, p. 1 (photograph) US National Archives bot/Wikimedia Commons; cover, p. 1 (succotash) Louella938/Shutterstock.com; p. 5 boreala/Shutterstock.com; pp. 6, 13 photo courtesy of Library of Congress; p. 7 Acacia217/Wikimedia Commons; p. 9 H. Armstrong Roberts/ClassicStock/ Archive Photos/Getty Images; p. 11 Natalie Fobes/Corbis Documentary/Getty Images; p. 12 Elovich/ Shutterstock.com; p. 14 Vladimir Volodin/Shutterstock.com; p. 15 Marilyn Angel Wynn/Corbis Documentary/Getty Images; pp. 17, 27 Marilyn Angel Wynn/Nativestock/Getty Images; p. 19 Judd Pilossof/Photolibrary/Getty Images; p. 20 Tillman/Wikimedia Commons; p. 21 Rudy Umans/Shutterstock.com; p. 23 Ralf Broskvar/Shutterstock.com; p. 24 matkub2499/Shutterstock.com; p. 25 Library of Congress/Contributor/Corbis Historical/Getty Images; p. 28 Mona Makela/ Shutterstock.com; p. 29 Harald Sund/The Image Bank/Getty Images.

Printed in the United States of America

CPSIA compliance information: Batch #CW18GS: For further information contact Gareth Stevens, New York, New York at 1-800-542-2595.

CONTENTS

Words in the glossary appear in **bold** type the first time they are used in the text.

EARLY PEOPLES OF NORTH AMERICA

When European settlers began arriving in North America in the 1500s, they found that Native Americans already lived across the land. There may have been as many as 240 native groups, sometimes called nations or tribes. Neighboring peoples shared similar ways of life, including what they ate and how they cooked.

The foods Native Americans ate depended on the plants and animals found in the area where they lived. Most Native Americans hunted, fished, and gathered wild plants. Others learned to farm.

Ancient Native American nations are often grouped based on where they lived and the cultural features they shared with their neighbors.

ARCTIC OCEAN

ARCTIC

NORTHWEST COAST

SUBARCTIC

PACIFIC OCEAN

PLATEAU

GREAT PLAINS

NORTHEAST

ATLANTIC OCEAN

GREAT BASIN

CALIFORNIA

SOUTHEAST

SOUTHWEST

MESOAMERICA

HUNTERS ON THE MOVE

Many Native American groups hunted animals, or game, such as deer and elk. Those living in the Great Plains area, such as the Sioux, were known for hunting large animals with humped backs called bison. Bison were found throughout the plains, feeding on grasses that grew there.

Some Plains peoples were nomadic. This means that they moved often, following a food source, rather than living in villages. Tracking and hunting bison became much easier after Spanish settlers brought horses to North America.

Bison were often hunted with bows and arrows. Sometimes, however, Native Americans would use teamwork to trick a herd into running off a cliff or falling into a pit.

DID YOU KNOW?

Native Americans often used as many parts of an animal as possible. Bison, for example, provided meat as well as bones for tools, hair for rope, and skins for clothing, blankets, and shelter.

TRAPPING SMALL GAME

Native Americans throughout North America hunted small game such as rabbits, squirrels, and ducks. Nations of the Great Basin—such as the Shoshone, Paiute, Ute, and Washoe—ate lizards, **rodents**, and snakes. In the Southeast, the Cherokee, Choctaw, Chickasaw, Creek, and Seminole ate otters, raccoons, and turkeys, among other animals.

Small game was hunted with nets, clubs, **spears**, and bows and arrows. Some peoples used traps. A snare is a type of trap that uses rope, wire, or string to catch an animal.

DID YOU KNOW?

Native Americans hunted ducks using decoys, or fake birds, they made from plants!

The Seminole of Florida hunted alligators and turtles for food.

FISHING FOR FOOD

Many Native Americans settled near bodies of water. Streams, rivers, lakes, and oceans provided much of their food. Some native groups, such as the Tlingit of the Northwest Coast, got most of their meat from fish, **crustaceans**, shellfish, seals, sea otters, and even whales.

One of the most common ways for Native Americans to catch fish was by jabbing at them with a spear. However, they also used nets, traps, and hooks made from animal bone.

DID YOU KNOW?

The Makah of today's Washington State used long spears called harpoons to hunt whales. Sometimes it took days to kill a whale. Then, its mouth was sewn shut to keep it from sinking. Finally, it was pulled ashore. The Makah still hunt whales.

Today, many Native Americans continue to fish. A Yakama man catches salmon with a net on the Klickitat River in Washington State.

GREAT GATHERERS

Hunting and fishing provided Native Americans with many kinds of meat. However, most groups gathered wild foods, too.

Native American gatherers collected nuts, seeds, roots, mushrooms, fruits, vegetables, and other types of plants. They were skilled at knowing which plants could be eaten and which were poisonous. Some of the plants were made into drinks and **medicines**. For example, the Santee Sioux and Ho-Chunk peoples of the Plains used garlic and onions to treat wounds.

GARLIC

DID YOU KNOW?

Native Americans also gathered honey, eggs, maple syrup, and salt.

The Pomo of California were hunter-gatherers.
This Pomo woman is shown collecting seeds in 1924.

13

ACORN FLOUR

Acorns were the most important food source for the Native Americans of California. These included the Hupa, Yurok, Pomo, Yuki, Wintun, Maidu, Miwok, and Yana. Acorns were easy to find in the surrounding forests. Women and children gathered them while men hunted and fished. Acorns were cracked and their insides ground into flour. This flour was used to make bread, soup, and other foods.

Acorns contain tannin, which is toxic. However, native peoples figured out how to remove the tannin from acorns with water.

Native Americans passed their cooking knowledge from parent to child. In this photo, a native family in California grinds acorns using stone tools.

LEARNING TO FARM

Nearly 9,000 years ago, Native Americans living in present-day Mexico figured out how to grow corn. This useful skill slowly spread across North America. The ability to grow crops meant Native Americans no longer had to be nomadic. They still hunted, but they also built settlements near their fields instead of chasing herds.

Early Native Americans of the Great Plains were hunters, gatherers, and farmers. They grew sunflowers, squash, beans, and corn. These were the **ancestors** of the Arikara, Mandan, Hidatsa, Crow, and Pawnee.

DID YOU KNOW?

Native Americans in hot, dry places, such as the Southwest, were able to farm, too. They created **irrigation** systems to move water from rivers and streams to fields.

The Cherokee people of the Southeast were excellent farmers. This picture shows a small Cherokee garden in Oklahoma, where many Cherokee now live.

17

TOP CROPS

Native Americans have depended on corn, beans, and squash as their main crops for thousands of years. Corn, also called maize, could be stored for a long time. It was grown in the summer, but eaten throughout the winter.

Maize, squash, and beans were often planted together because they helped each other grow. Corn plants held up bean vines, bean plants made the soil rich, and squash leaves helped keep water in the soil. Together, these plants were called the "three sisters."

DID YOU KNOW?

Other important Native American crops included tomatoes, potatoes, peppers, and wild rice, which is a kind of grass.

Succotash is a **traditional** Native American dish of Southeast peoples. Made mostly from corn and beans, it's still eaten today.

TOOLS OF THE TRADE

Native Americans looked to nature for cooking **utensils**, too. A *metate* was a smooth stone upon which maize was placed. Another stone, called a *mano*, was used to grind the maize. These tools were used in the Southwest more than 1,500 years ago.

Jars, bowls, and other containers were made from stone or baked clay. Some Native Americans, such as the Hupa and Maidu of California, **wove** grasses tightly into baskets. These baskets could even be used for boiling water.

MANO

METATE

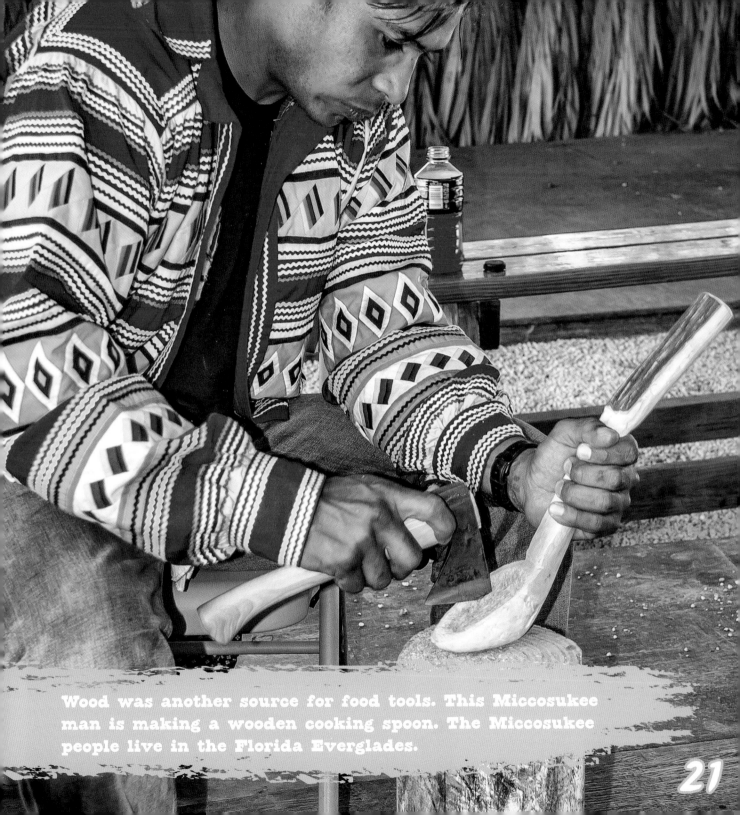

Wood was another source for food tools. This Miccosukee man is making a wooden cooking spoon. The Miccosukee people live in the Florida Everglades.

COOKING WITH FIRE

Native Americans throughout North America used fire to cook, sometimes outside their homes. They had a number of methods to prepare food, including baking, grilling, roasting, smoking, boiling, and steaming.

Some Native Americans dug pits in which they heated stones with fire. Food was grilled on top of the hot stones, or the stones were used to heat food inside baskets. Native Americans in the Southwest used an outdoor clay oven called an horno (OHR-noh) to cook their food. Some still bake bread this way.

DID YOU KNOW?

Native Americans enjoyed simple, fresh meals. They didn't use many spices. Some food, such as fish, was smoked or dried, which allowed it to be stored and eaten later.

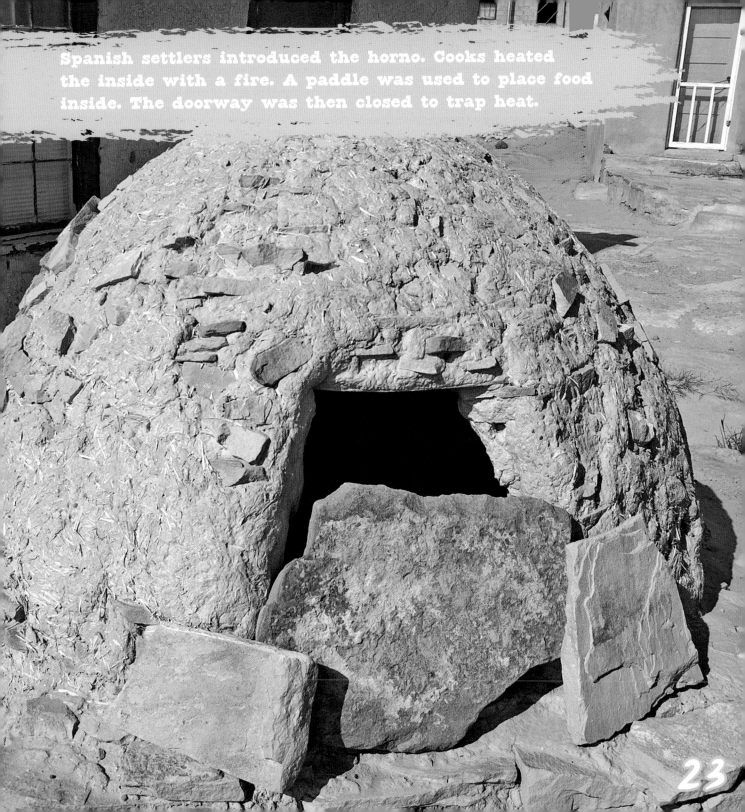

Spanish settlers introduced the horno. Cooks heated the inside with a fire. A paddle was used to place food inside. The doorway was then closed to trap heat.

23

FOODS AND CELEBRATIONS

Some Native American groups used food as part of their **religions**. The Comanche of the Great Plains raised a piece of food in the air and then burned it to show thanks to the Creator God for their feast.

Native Americans also used food for **celebrations**. Many held feasts that lasted several days in thanksgiving for their crops. Some Native Americans in the Southeast continue to celebrate the Green Corn Festival in late July or August when the corn is ripe.

DID YOU KNOW?

The Creek people of the Southeast started their new year when their maize started to ripen.

To share the wealth of a good crop, Native Americans of the Pacific Northwest held a feast called a potlatch, in which goods and foods were given to guests. Some groups still do.

CHANGING THE WORLD

When Christopher Columbus arrived in the Americas in 1492, Native Americans were growing more than 200 different types of maize. Columbus took maize back to Europe, and it spread from there.

Many other Native American foods were also shared around the world. Fruits such as blueberries, cranberries, and black raspberries first came from North America. Wild rice, pumpkins, and other types of squash did, too. People everywhere were soon eating these new foods, thanks to native peoples.

DID YOU KNOW?

People around the world still use some native cooking methods, such as cooking salmon on pieces of cedar wood.

Food historians think about 60 percent of the food eaten around the world was originally from the Americas.

27

NATIVE AMERICAN TASTES TODAY

Just as Europeans were introduced to new foods in North America, they brought new food sources, including wheat, cows, and sheep. Native Americans adopted these into their cultures.

Most Native Americans today live quite differently than their ancestors did. Many buy their food at stores. Even those who still farm, such as the Navajo of the Southwest, grow European crops along with their traditional ones. Learning about—and eating—native foods is a great way to celebrate Native American cultures.

Fry bread is a traditional food still enjoyed by many Native Americans today. This simple bread is made with flour, water, baking powder, and salt.

GLOSSARY

ancestor: a person in someone's family who lived in past times

celebration: a party or other special event for an important occasion

crustacean: a type of animal, such as a crab or lobster, that has several pairs of legs and a body made up of sections covered in a hard outer shell

cultural: having to do with the beliefs and ways of life of a group of people

irrigation: the watering of a dry area by man-made means in order to grow plants

medicine: something used in treating illness or reducing pain

religion: the belief in a god or gods

rodent: a small animal, such as a mouse, rat, squirrel, or beaver, that has sharp front teeth

spear: a long wooden stick with a sharp point

traditional: having to do with long-practiced ways of life

utensil: a simple and helpful tool used for doing tasks in a home, especially in the kitchen

weave: to make something by crossing long pieces of material over and under each other

FOR MORE INFORMATION

BOOKS

Beckett, Leslie. *Native American Recipes*. New York, NY: KidHaven Publishing, 2017.

Dennis, Yvonne Wakim. *A Kid's Guide to Native American History: More Than 50 Activities*. Chicago, IL: Chicago Review Press, 2010.

Smithyman, Kathryn. *Native North American Foods and Recipes*. New York, NY: Crabtree Publishing, 2006.

WEBSITES

Native American Food
www.historyforkids.net/native-american-food.html
Visit this site to learn what Native Americans ate and how they prepared their meals.

Native Americans: Agriculture and Food
www.ducksters.com/history/native_american_agriculture_food.php
Find out more about how Native Americans hunted, gathered, and farmed their food.

INDEX